Make a Foothold & Skyrocket your Stationery Business

REBUILD

7 Steps to Strong Foundation for a Successful Stationery Business

Make a Foothold & Skyrocket your Stationery Business

REBUILD

7 Steps to Strong Foundation for a Successful Stationery Business

ARUN ARORA

Worldwide Publishing by

Pendown Press

Powered by Gullybaba.com

PENDOWN PRESS

Powered by **Gullybaba Publishing House Pvt. Ltd.**,
An ISO 9001 & ISO 14001 Certified Co.,
Regd. Office: 2525/193, 1st Floor, Onkar Nagar-A, Tri Nagar,
Delhi-110035
Ph.: 09350849407, 09312235086
E-mail: info@pendownpress.com
Branch Office: 1A/2A, 20, Hari Sadan, Ansari Road,
Daryaganj, New Delhi-110002
Ph.: 011-45794768
Website: PendownPress.com

First Edition: 2021

ISBN: 978-93-90557-88-2

All Rights Reserved

All the ideas and thoughts in this book are given by the author and he is responsible for the treatise, facts and dialogues used in this book. He is also responsible for the used pictures and the permission to use them in this book. Copyright of this book is reserved with the author. The publisher does not have any responsibility for the above-mentioned matters. No part of this publication may be reproduced, distributed, or transmitted in any form or by any means, including photocopying, recording, or other electronic or mechanical methods, without the prior written permission of the publisher and author.

Layout and Cover Designed by Pendown Graphics Team
Printed and Bound in India by Thomson Press India Ltd.

CONTENTS

About Me

[Page-i]

Chapter 1
Treat Your Shop as a Brand

[Page-1]

Chapter 2
What is Your USP?

[Page-3]

Chapter 3
Marketing–Your Business' Game Changer

[Page-5]

Chapter 4
Money is in the List

[Page-9]

Chapter 5
Jo Dikhta Hai Vo Bikta Hai, Boss

[Page-13]

Chapter 6
Digitize Your Business

[Page-17]

Chapter 7
Selling is not the only Purpose, Adding Value is!

[Page-19]

Chapter 8
Let's Recap

[Page-21]

ABOUT THE AUTHOR

Hello,

I am Arun Arora, Managing Director & CEO of World One, India's leading file manufacturing company. I am committed to deliver the finest products and share all my learnings, through this book, to benefit stationery retailers in India.

My journey with stationery industry began three decades ago. After completing my education, I joined my uncle's business of file manufacturing in the stationery hub of Delhi-Chawri Bazar. I was fascinated to find so many varieties of stationery articles. I, somewhere, saw the possibility to innovate and create exciting products in this industry segment. It was a moment that I cannot forget. Deep down I knew that this is exactly what I want to do.

Today, I live stationery with every breath of my life.

I have been lucky to work with many big retailers and stationery manufacturers across the globe including the world's biggest retailer Walmart; I have learnt a lot from them. In 2013, we were awarded the "Best Partner Award" in office supply category by none other than Walmart.

While working in this industry, I have observed that most Indian stationers start business in a conventional way. They don't have much clarity on vision and the processes involved. And it's okay when you are working your way up the ladder. As time flows business starts to grow, so are the problems associated with it.

I have noticed that there are some common problems that stationers face. Given below are some of these problems:

1. Stationers need to handle a huge number of items, somewhere between 10,000 -15,0000 different SKUs as this industry is vast with so many options of products.

2. By and large, **stationers are one-man army**, handling almost every function (purchase/sales/operations) of business by themselves leaving them stressed and burned out. On top of it, in many cases the next generation is not willing to join their business.

3. Training the right manpower is a consistent challenge.

4. There is always a space crunch to display the products due to huge number of SKUs.

5. Physical inventories are often mismatched with records.

6. The inventory/sales ratio is very high which result in more capital requirement to run the business.

7. Net profits usually touch the bottom due to high competition.

If you are a stationer and facing even one of the above problems, then this INSTABOOK is for you.

Now, you must be wondering that why am I sharing all these years of my expertise and hacks that I learnt with pain and hard work for FREE?

So, Here is WHY…

One, I am in love with stationery trade and it pains my heart when I see stationers struggling to manage their business due to lack of knowledge.

Two, due to time and geographical constraints, I may not be able to meet each one of you personally and share my understandings and knowledge that I have gained over the years. This e-book is my small gift to stationery retail owners and startups.

I hope these seven chapters will add a lot more value to your business and will help you gain insights on the profitability in it.

Your trustworthy file folders manufacturer and a stationery retail expert.

–Arun Arora

CHAPTER 1

TREAT YOUR SHOP AS A BRAND

*"A brand is a voice and
a product is a souvenir."*

–Lisa Gansky

Whether you are a first-generation entrepreneur or you joined the legacy of your parents/grandparents, I know you love your shop. Day and night you are thinking on how to take your business to the next level. It is this shop which has given you the recognition and respect apart from earning livelihood for you and your team.

Do you know your shop's name is so powerful that it is imprinted on your customers' minds for years. Your customers see your shop as a trusted, convenient and preferred place to buy their stationery needs. They see, remember and talk about it as a famous stationery shop in their area. It's high time you start seeing your shop as a Brand and nurture it to make it the most preferred stationery shop of your area.

Let's understand the deep-rooted benefits of positioning your shop as a brand through a few examples:

Crossword, a famous book shop, started in 1992, positioned itself as a brand. It was a time, when the books were usually sold through unorganised retail book Shop & Customers usually have to wait long time to buy. It designed its shop in a way so that customers get a greater experience when they come to buy the books. When people visit and buy a book from Crossword, they don't bargain, they just select the book and get it billed. You may have experienced the same when you had visited a Kirana shop versus some branded store like Reliance Fresh. You may bargain at your local Kirana shop but you never do that at the branded grocery stores like Reliance Fresh or Spencers.

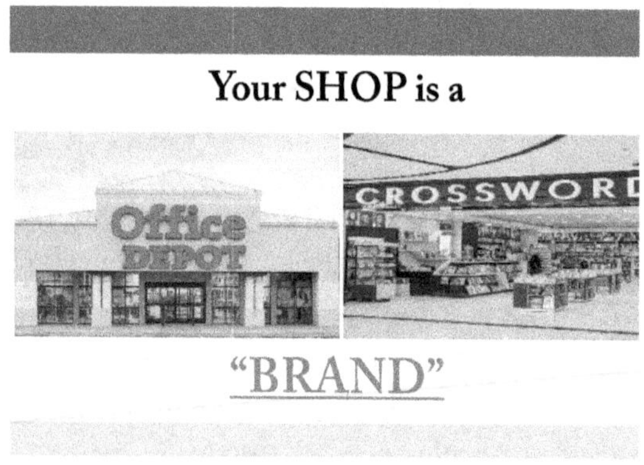

If you don't create a brand, you will be treated as a commodity just like any product, and believe me, you will always have a challenge associated with commoditization. Brand brings value and trust to you and your customers.

Visualize and market your shop as a Brand.

CHAPTER 2

WHAT IS YOUR USP?

"If you don't distinguish yourself from the crowd, you'll just be the crowd."

–Rebecca Mark

How does your customers recognise you?

Ever thought of asking this question to yourself? Every establishment/brand has its own strength. You should find it out and develop your USP (Unique Selling Proposition) around it. It's like finding and telling your specialization to your customers. People love to buy from experts.

For example, if you have pain in your eyes, will you prefer to consult an eye specialist or a general physician? Of course an eye specialist! Similarly, your customer should know about your area of specialization.

You can ask these questions to yourself:

Are you a famous book shop?

Are you famous as an art material expert?

Is your store famous for wonderful shopping experience with a lot of innovative stationery products?

Are you famous for lowest price in the town?

Are you famous as school books and stationery expert?

Are you a professional office supplier?

Discover your strength, nurture and publicize it to imprint in your customers' mind.

Ever wonder, even the "Chhole Bhature" (Punjab's famous regional food) eatery becomes the talk of the town and gets attention of the media too.

You must remember to speak out loud about your specialization to create your USP and stand out of the competition.

What are known for?

In which Category can you be The number One?

Today in brand World One, we sell so many stationery products but we are mainly known as an expert of Files and Folders. So, don't get confused when I ask you to develop a USP of your brand. You can sell as many products as you can handle. Just specialize in something and get known for that.

Think, in which category you can be number one?

STAND OUT!! Create your own USP.

CHAPTER 3

MARKETING–YOUR BUSINESS' GAME CHANGER

*"Marketing done right eliminates
or reduces the need of sales."*

–Peter Drucker

I know you have been working hard to establish your shop as a famous brand with a particular USP. From morning to evening you are busy in operations and products to justify your USP. You get so busy in bringing exciting products in your store and in managing the day-to-day operations that you forget to invite your customers to your shop, to delight them with the best you have brought for them!

It's like you are doing your best efforts to organize a wedding ceremony of your child—decorations all done, best food is prepared, but you forgot to invite the guests!

Marketing, in business, is inviting more and more customers to your shop, more than you can handle.

A study shows that an average entrepreneur spends 65% of his time in operations, 25% in products and only 10% in marketing. However, for the robust growth it's recommended for an entrepreneur to spend 65% of his time in marketing, 25% in product and only 10% in operations.

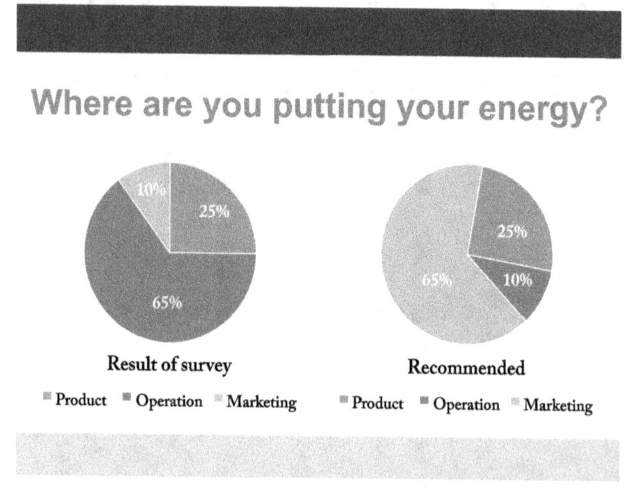

Most of small business neglect this major aspect of business. It's like having a Mercedes car with lots of accessories fitted but with no engine… and you really sweat a lot pushing it to move (doesn't it remind you of what you are doing in your business… pushing it throughout your life). Marketing in business is like engine in car. You need to market your shop to create a pull that can bring more and more people to your business.

<u>Marketing</u>

To Bring More Customer To Your Store

Marketing is a Game Changer, Remember this!!

Important: Don't confuse selling with marketing.

Selling is like serving a guest who has come to the marriage and marketing is like inviting them to the marriage.

CHAPTER 4

MONEY IS IN THE LIST

Having understood the importance of marketing, you might be thinking as to how is it possible for a small business to do the marketing? Only the big businesses can do it; they have a lot of money to spend on ads on TV, radio, newspapers, hoardings, etc.

Brother, today, I will tell you how to market your shop without spending a penny and get the customers lined up at your shop, and increase the revenue by more than 100%.

Are you interested to know this secret?

Many among us have a shop operational for last 5-10 years, and some of you might be running your ancestral shops which could be 25-100 year old. My question is: have you ever made a list of people who have been visiting your shop and noted their contact details?

Majority of stationers nod in a no, when I ask them. Because most of the shops do the transactional business with customers and never bother to record their contact details to remain connected with them. Don't you agree that if you invite your old customers to your shop they will feel happy and privileged, and would like to shop more from you?

Your List Includes

- Existing Customers
- Unconverted Leads
- Past Customers
- Database You Own / Bought
- Business Cards
- Fans & Followers on Social Media Platform

Let me tell you one example to show the power of list.

There was a small pizza shop in a town which used to make very good pizzas. One day, a person after having a pizza from that eatery asked him how he is getting the customers to his shop. The eatery owner said he spends a lot on marketing through Facebook, radio, posters, hordings and newspapers. The person said, "brother, what if I tell you a way which will cost you a penny, but gets you more business than what all other channels bring to you? Will you be interested to know?" The pizza shop owner said, "YES off course, please bring it on."

"Today onwards, start making a list of customers who order pizzas from your place and record their contact details in your system. After a month, start sending them some offers and information of new pizzas/dishes that you make. Keep a separate phone to record the orders received through the list and other marketing channels," the person advised and left.

After few months the person visited that Pizza shop again and asked the owner how is his business going? The owner was amazed with the results. He told that he was getting double the orders from the list than any other channels and that he has stopped spending a hefty amount on the ads. There is already an increase in his business' profitability by 4 times.

I want to ask you - why are you digging a well everyday to get a glass of water when a well you already dug can give you water for life-long?

Simple Math

Assuming an average lifetime value of stationery consumer is ₹3,00,000 (3 lac)

Value of one name in the list is ₹3,00,000 (3 lac)

Value of 100 names in the list is ₹300000x100=₹300,00,000 (3 crore)

Value of 1000 names in the list is ₹300000x1000= ₹30,00,00,000 (30 crores)

Value of 10000 names in a list is ₹300000x10000= ₹300,00,00,000 (300 crore)

And so on.....

After running a shop for so many years, how many people are in your list? The number of customers in your list determines the value of your business.

Today, the companies are valued on the basis of their active customer base. Start making a list and RE-invite your customers to your shop.

The Money is in the LIST! Activate it !!!

CHAPTER 5

JO DIKHTA HAI VO BIKTA HAI, BOSS

Friends, you will surely agree to the old saying *'jo dikhta hai vo bikta hai'* and the same can be experienced from the fact that we end up shopping much more than required from a store where products are displayed in a scientific manner.

Merchandise rightly displayed increases the visibility and, hence, the ticket size of your customers. It is also a good reason for a customer to visit your store more often to explore the products

fulfilling their needs and unrealized needs (desires). I get disappointed when I hear from the customers that they feel hard to find any innovation and excitement in shopping for stationery in India & they usually buy it a lot when they travel abroad. It's contradictory! On one hand, stationers are handling 10,000 to

15,000 products and on the other hand, the customers don't find any innovation and excitement in shopping for stationery in India. The reason is, usually retailers fill their shelves like a warehouse, thereby, decreasing the visibility of products resulting in low shopping experience and low ticket size.

Merchandising & displaying a product is an art as well as science. The right merchandise displayed at right place, at right time, in right quantity and at right price can result in a great shopping experience and increase in sales.

5 Easy Ways to Increase Sales with Visual Merchandising

#1. Display Category wise

Display made according to the product category increases the chances of customer buying more related products. For example, if you display all tapes, adhesives and allied items at one place there are chances that customers who come to buy a tape, also buy a tape dispenser. You must have noticed that when you buy a mobile phone from an e-commerce portal, it recommends you related products like mobile covers and accessories. Because of this you end up buying more things than you had planned.

#2. Keep an Eye on Height

Displays that showcase items at eye level attract more attention than the ones that force a customer to look down or up. The average eye level is approximately 61 inches measured from the floor. Display the new arrivals and more profitable items at eye level.

#3. Practise the Rule of Three

Friends, it's a big myth that sales increases by keeping more options of a product serving a purpose. Scientifically, more than 3 choices for a purpose confuses the customer and reduces the probability of sales. Merchandising is an art, to select the SKUs based on certain criteria to fulfill the varied demands of customers and at same time restricting the duplication of items serving the same purpose.

#4. Clear Price Point Placement

Customers generally don't like asking for a price or having to spend time searching for the price. Clear price points on displays or products enhance the shopping comfort.

#5. Bring in the excitement of New

Mark the new arrivals, the categories with pop-up signs. It brings fresh energy and excitement in the store.

CHAPTER 6

DIGITIZE YOUR BUSINESS

As a passionate entrepreneur, I am sure, you might always be on the lookout for different ways to make your customer's life easy. After Covid-19 pandemic, the world entered the low touch economy and many of your customers want their needs to be delivered at home. The lack of digitization in business is diverting them to others stores/platforms which offer convenience of online shopping, digital payments and home deliveries.

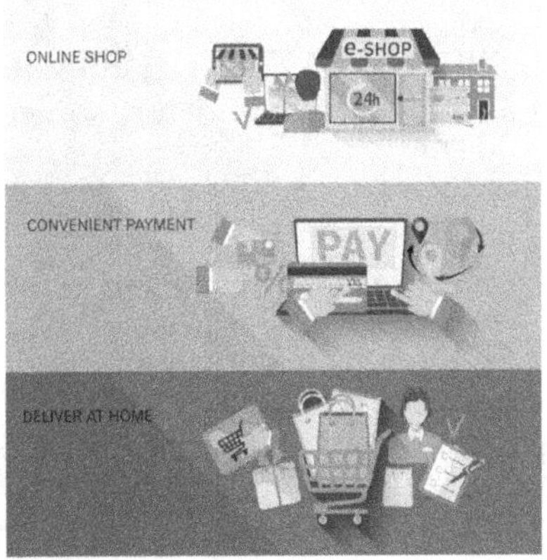

Over the last 10 years with the boom of e-commerce, we have seen almost everything—from cloths to electronics—delivered at our home.

When a nearby restaurant can deliver a cooked food at home, then the stationery could be no exception. The e-shop concept is a new avatar of e-commerce. It helps you take your store digital to sell and reconnect with your customers digitally. Here approach makes the difference. E-commerce platforms like Amazon and Flipkart have a transactional approach for business. There the seller has hardly any relationship with customer; however, the e-shop concept helps you to connect with your customers at deeper level. In this model, both you and your customers know each other and they can connect & buy from you with the same confidence as they buy from your shop. There is warmth of relationship and trust.

There are so many inexpensive tools like Whatsapp, Facebook and Instagram to keep a connect with your customers.

It's high time you start digitizing your business and acquire this new skill of connecting &selling online to give your customers the convenience of shopping from their places.

Remember: Your customers are looking for you in a digital world, you need to bridge this gap before someone else.

SELLING IS NOT THE ONLY PURPOSE, ADDING VALUE IS!

*"People buy people first
and then their product or services."*

Do you want your customers to buy from you always despite the competitions? Do you feel your profit margins are shrinking day by day due to both online and offline competitions?

If the answer of any one of the above question is yes then this Chapter is written exclusively for you!

Ever wondered why we visit the same family doctor every time we get ill? Why do we visit same salon and prefer to get the haircut by the same barber? Why do we prefer to buy gold from a shop from where we are buying since long time? There is a warm relationship and high trust in all the above examples. If you look deeper, you will find that you developed trust/relationship with them as they added value to your life over a period of time. By having a relevant communication over a period of time and giving super high value information or advice which will provide immense benefit to your customers, you build a warm relationship and a buying environment.

When you add massive value to your customers' lives, they develop a warm relationship and a high trust with you. You became the default choice in their subconscious minds. They see you as an expert and value your recommendations. Price becomes secondary to them as they strongly believe to get the best value from you,ONLY.

Create a buying environment. People buy on emotions & then justify on intellect.

CHAPTER 8

LET'S RECAP

1. Treat your shop as a Brand

2. What is your USP?

3. Marketing—Your Business' Game Changer

4. Money is in the List

5. *Jo dikhta hai vo bikta hai*

6. Digitalize your Business

7. Selling is not the only purpose, adding value is!

You have 2 choices

As you have reached this Chapter's end, I must congratulate you on your perseverance and willingness to make a change in your life and business. It shows that you have some level of commitment and want to make an effort for your business to succeed, and that you're willing to take action to Rebuild your stationery business to make it more profitable and take it to the next level.

Here, you have two choices—one you go and identify all roadblocks that are there in your system and then you go ahead and solve them. I have imparted knowledge to you and using this new understanding, you can do it yourself.

The second option is to have me by your side. I will do a complete analysis of where your problem is in your system and will hand-hold you to identify and resolve it.

We can do this over a cup of tea at my office or via a video call.

I will give you some solutions there and then, and make a plan to resolve some deep rooted one.

To book an appointment, send your interest by Whatsapp message on 9310404460 or by email at support@rebuildclub.com

Looking forward to meet you.

Warm Regards

–Arun Arora

Your trustworthy Stationery Manufacturer
& Retail Expert

www.ingramcontent.com/pod-product-compliance
Lightning Source LLC
LaVergne TN
LVHW022057190726
843495LV00014B/1795